PEGASUS

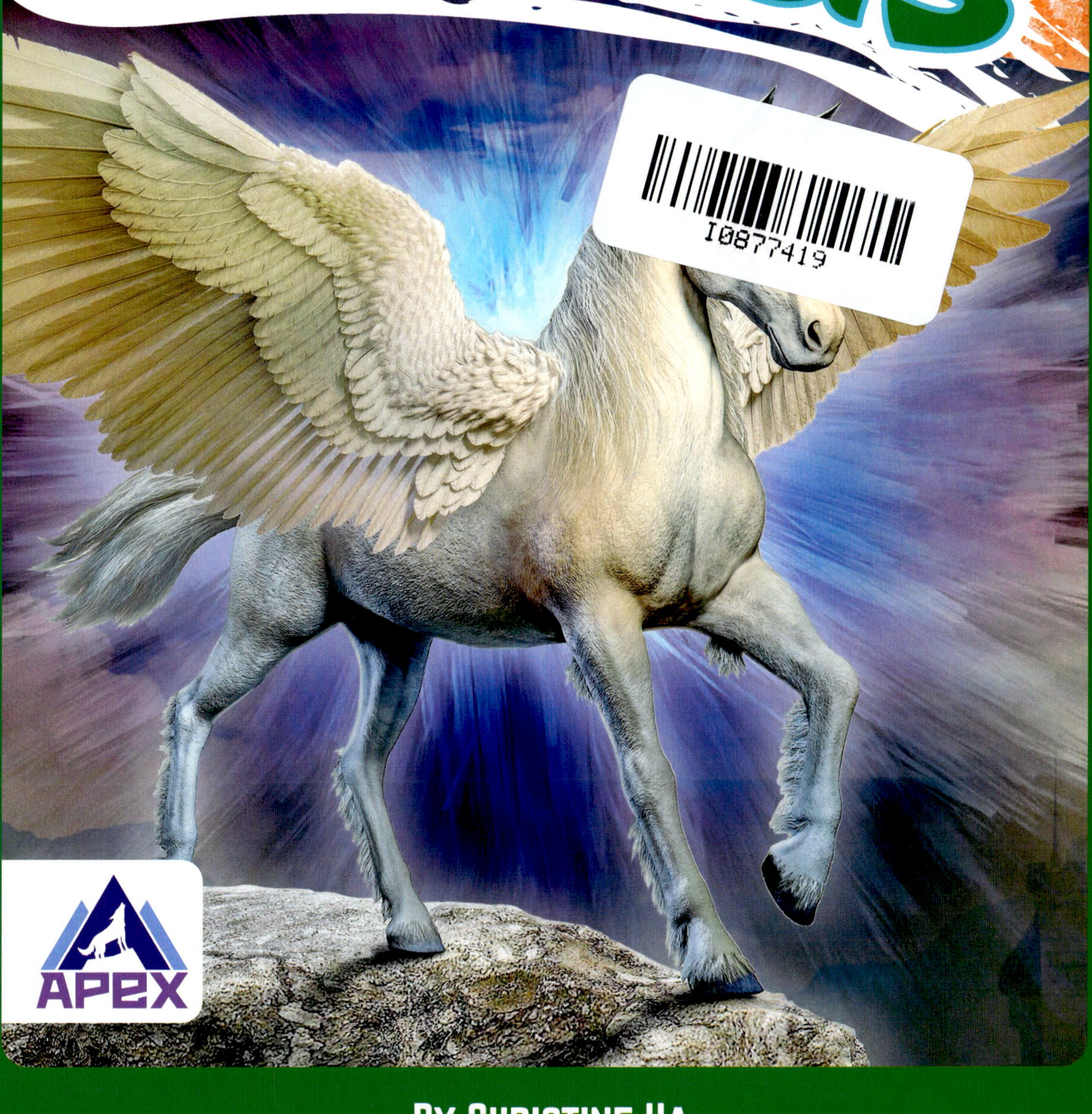

APEX

BY CHRISTINE HA

WWW.APEXEDITIONS.COM

Apex is distributed by North Star Editions:
sales@northstareditions.com | 888-417-0195

Produced for Apex by Red Line Editorial.

Photographs ©: iStockphoto, cover, 1, 8–9, 10–11, 16–17, 20, 27, 29; Shutterstock Images, 4–5, 6–7, 12–13, 14, 15, 18–19, 21, 22–23, 24–25, 26

Library of Congress Control Number: 2020952923

ISBN
978-1-63738-022-2 (hardcover)
978-1-63738-058-1 (paperback)
978-1-63738-127-4 (ebook pdf)
978-1-63738-094-9 (hosted ebook)

Printed in the United States of America
Mankato, MN
082021

NOTE TO PARENTS AND EDUCATORS

Apex books are designed to build literacy skills in striving readers. Exciting, high-interest content attracts and holds readers' attention. The text is carefully leveled to allow students to achieve success quickly. Additional features, such as bolded glossary words for difficult terms, help build comprehension.

TABLE OF CONTENTS

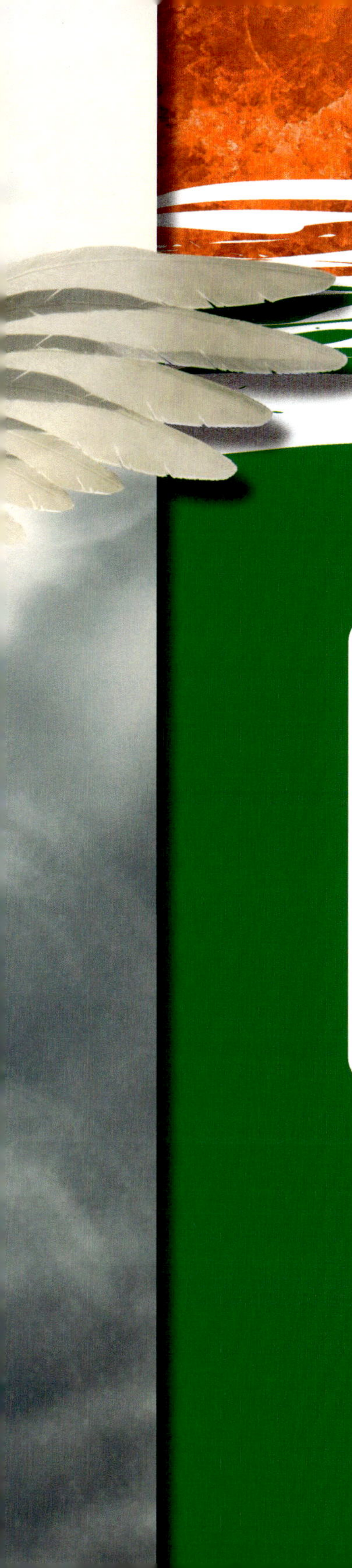

CHAPTER 1

INTO THE SKY

A hero walks through the forest. He is looking for Pegasus. He finds the white horse by a small pond. Its wings shine in the sun.

In art, Pegasus often has snow-white hair.

In stories, heroes often save people from monsters.

The hero needs to **defeat** a monster. He asks Pegasus to help. Pegasus nods. It lets the hero climb onto its back.

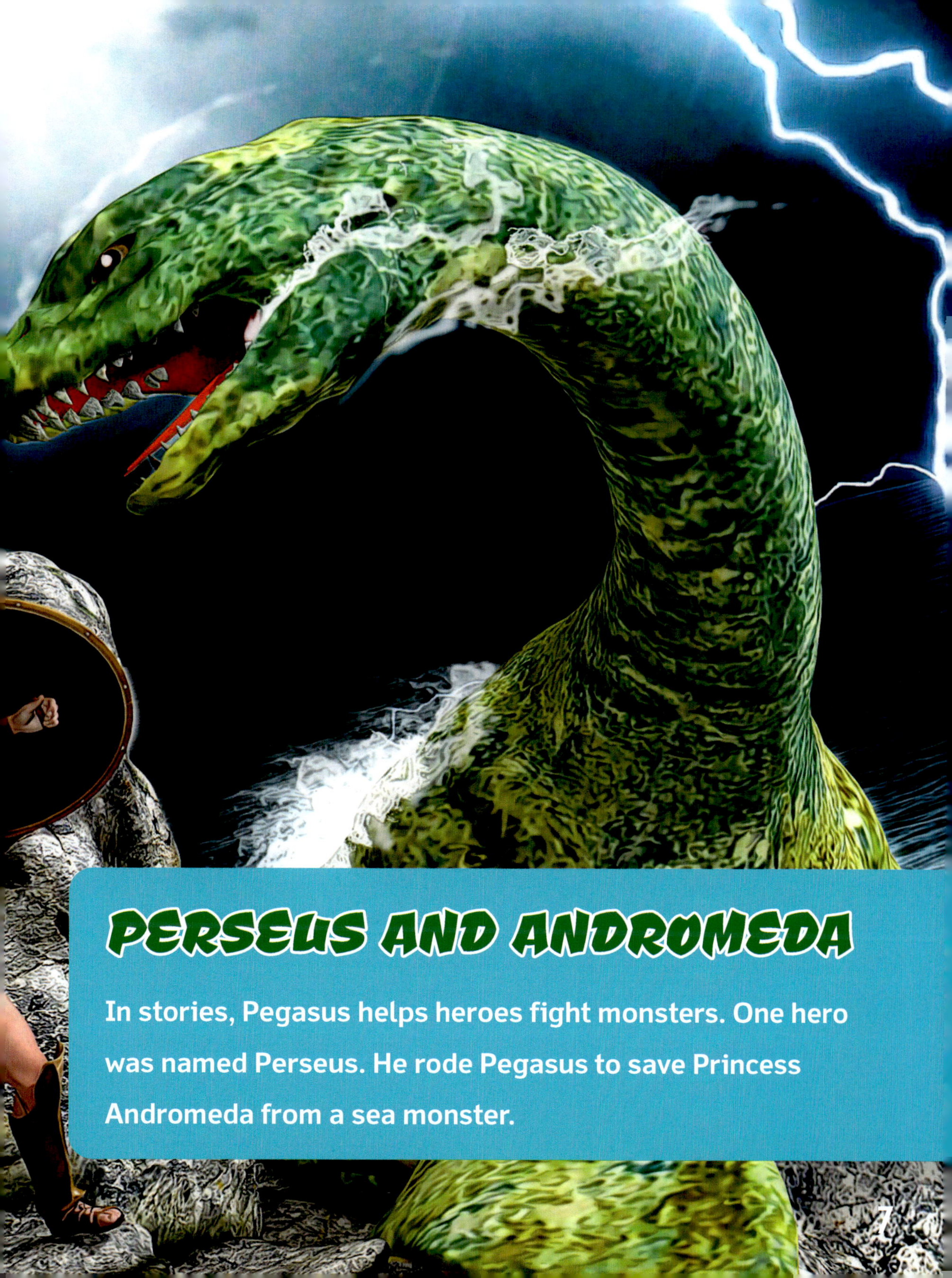

PERSEUS AND ANDROMEDA

In stories, Pegasus helps heroes fight monsters. One hero was named Perseus. He rode Pegasus to save Princess Andromeda from a sea monster.

Pegasus is often a symbol of strength and speed.

The winged horse starts running. Then it leaps into the air. The hero and the horse soar through the sky. They fly off to fight the monster.

In addition to flying, Pegasus can run very fast on the ground.

CHAPTER 2

WINGED HORSE

Pegasus is a magical horse with wings. It comes from Greek **mythology**. Pegasus has a white coat. Its mane and tail are white, too.

Austria's Mirabell Gardens features a sculpture of a leaping Pegasus.

Pegasus was related to Medusa. She was a monster with snakes for hair. Pegasus was born from her blood when a hero killed her.

Medusa had the power to turn anyone who looked at her into stone.

Pegasus's father was Poseidon, the Greek god of the sea.

At first, Pegasus was wild and free. Later, a hero tamed it. The hero's name was Bellerophon. He and Pegasus had many adventures.

Bellerophon rode Pegasus to attack enemies from above.

Legends say some springs give power to people who drink or bathe in their water.

SPRING MAKER

Pegasus can create **springs** by stomping its hoof. One famous spring is on Mount Helicon. Its water is said to help poets be **creative**.

CHAPTER 3

A HERO'S HORSE

Pegasus helped Bellerophon win fights. In one, he killed the Chimera. This monster had three heads. It could also breathe fire.

Bellerophon stabbed the Chimera to kill it.

Some stories say Pegasus belonged to the Muses. These goddesses helped people make art.

But Bellerophon became too proud. He tried flying to Mount Olympus. This was where the gods lived. The gods got angry. They sent a fly to bite Pegasus.

Some stories say Pegasus helped the goddess Eos bring the dawn.

The horse bucked Bellerophon. He fell back to the earth. But Pegasus stayed with the gods. It carried Zeus's lightning and thunder.

Zeus is the ruler of the Greek gods. He controls lightning and thunder.

Several constellations get their names from Greek myths.

IN THE STARS

A **constellation** is named after Pegasus. In Greece, these stars first appear at the end of summer. This marks the beginning of thunderstorm season.

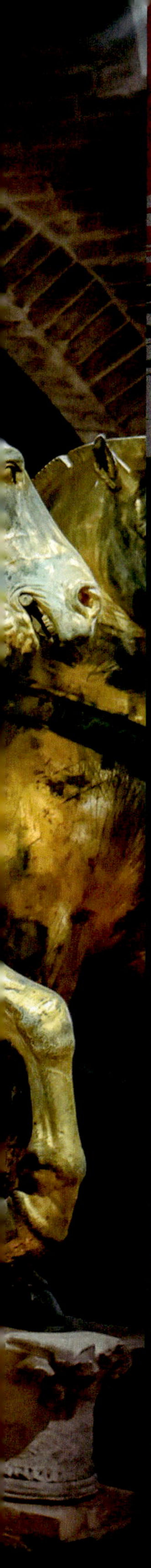

CHAPTER 4

HORSES IN LEGENDS

In ancient Greece, horses were **valuable**. They had many uses. People used them to hunt, fight, and travel. Horses also cost a lot. Owning one was a sign of **status**.

Horses appear in ancient art from around the world.

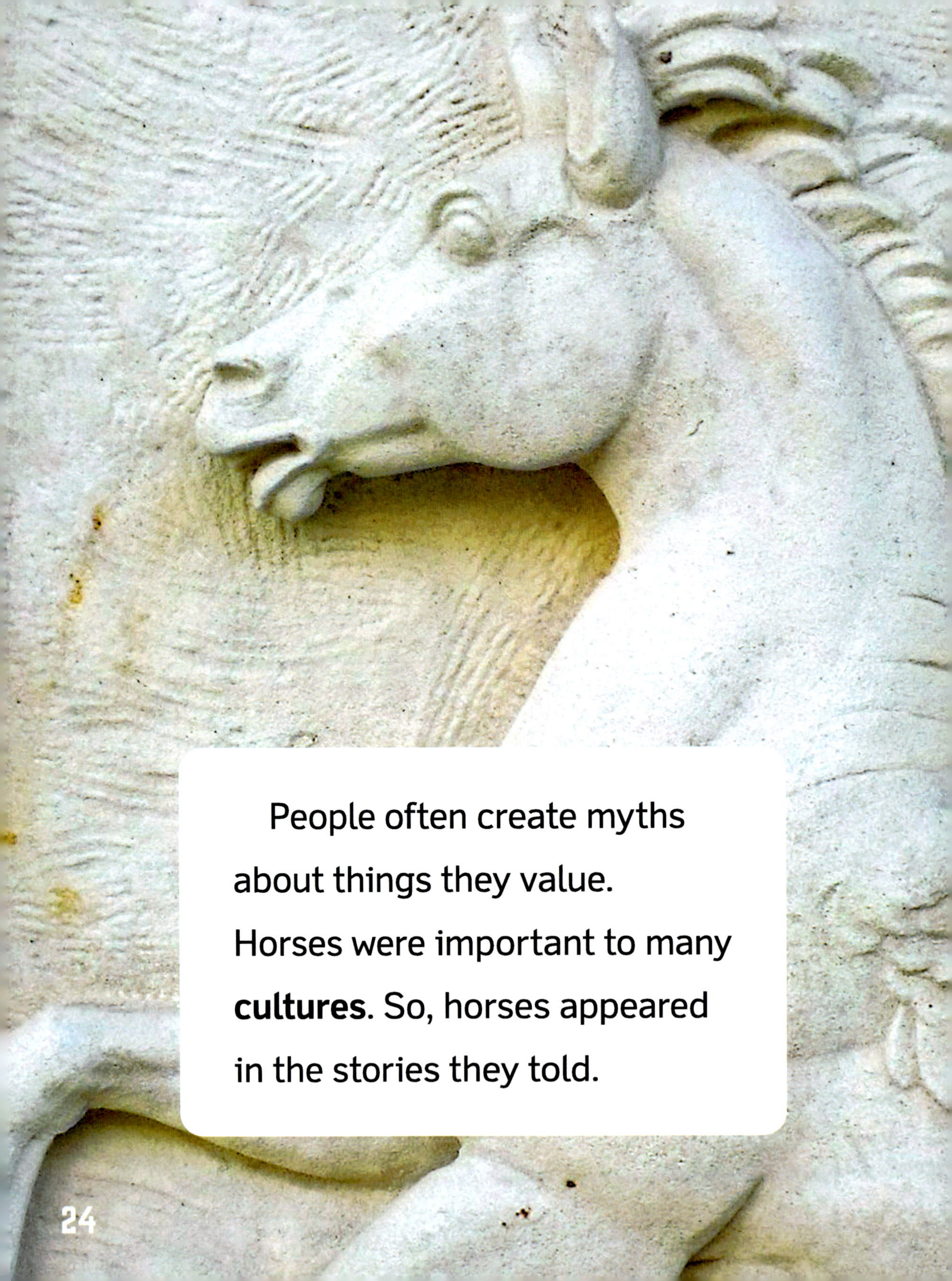

People often create myths about things they value. Horses were important to many **cultures**. So, horses appeared in the stories they told.

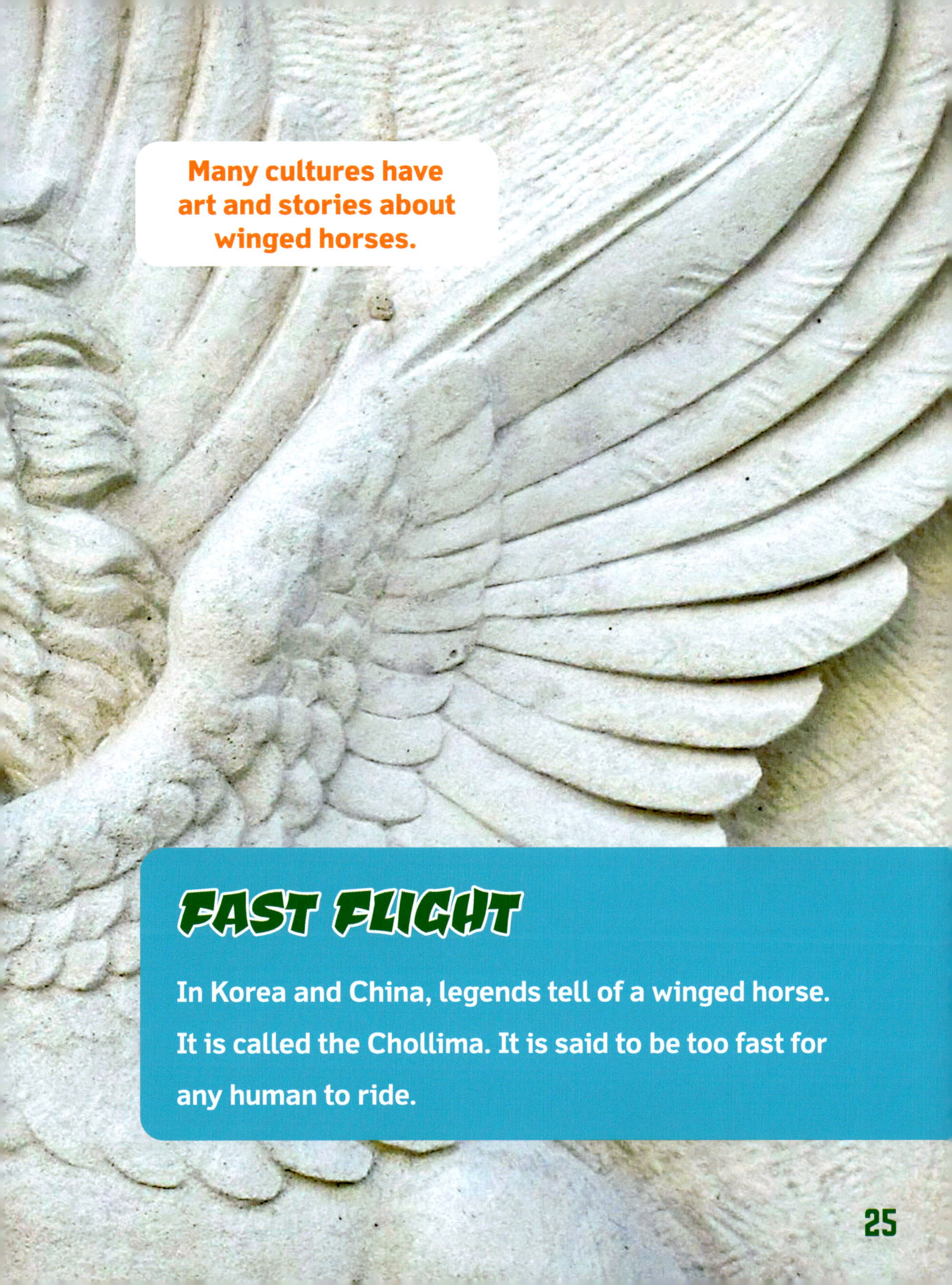

Many cultures have art and stories about winged horses.

FAST FLIGHT

In Korea and China, legends tell of a winged horse. It is called the Chollima. It is said to be too fast for any human to ride.

Greek myths tell of several magical horses. Pegasus is one of them. Others are said to pull **chariots** for the gods.

Pegasus appears on many coins from ancient Greece.

A hippocampus is half horse and half fish.

In Greek myths, the god Ares has four magical horses. They can breathe fire.

COMPREHENSION QUESTIONS

Write your answers on a separate piece of paper.

1. Write a paragraph that describes the key ideas of Chapter 3.
2. Would you want to ride on Pegasus? Why or why not?
3. Who tried to ride Pegasus to Mount Olympus?
   - **A.** Bellerophon
   - **B.** Perseus
   - **C.** Medusa
4. Why would owning a horse be a sign of status?
   - **A.** Buying a horse did not cost much.
   - **B.** Buying a horse was not possible in Greece.
   - **C.** Buying a horse showed a person had lots of money.

5. What does **tamed** mean in this book?

*At first, Pegasus was wild and free. Later, a hero **tamed** it.*

A. trained an animal to be less wild
B. fought against an animal
C. made an animal more wild

6. What does **soar** mean in this book?

*The hero and the horse **soar** through the sky. They fly off to fight the monster.*

A. to hold very still
B. to stay on the ground
C. to fly high in the air

Answer key on page 32.

GLOSSARY

chariots
Two-wheeled carts pulled by horses or other animals.

constellation
A group of stars that form a shape.

creative
Able to make art or come up with new ideas.

cultures
Groups of people and the ways they live, including their beliefs and laws.

defeat
To beat in a fight or contest.

mythology
A culture's traditional stories that explain the world in some way.

springs
Places where water bubbles up from underground.

status
How rich or important a person is, especially compared to other people.

valuable
Very important or worth lots of money.

TO LEARN MORE

BOOKS

Buckey, A. W. *Greek Gods, Heroes, and Mythology.* Minneapolis: Abdo Publishing, 2019.

Owings, Lisa. *Unicorns.* Minneapolis: Bellwether Media, 2021.

Sautter, A. J. *Discover Harpies, Minotaurs, and Other Mythical Fantasy Beasts.* North Mankato, MN: Capstone Press, 2018.

ONLINE RESOURCES

Visit **www.apexeditions.com** to find links and resources related to this title.

ABOUT THE AUTHOR

Christine Ha lives in Minnesota. She enjoys reading mythology and urban legends from around the world.

INDEX

Answer Key:
1. Answers will vary; **2.** Answers will vary; **3.** A; **4.** C; **5.** A; **6.** C